Dr Johnson's Doorknob

DR JOHNSON'S DOORKNOB

AND OTHER SIGNIFICANT PARTS OF
GREAT MEN'S HOUSES

*

LIZ WORKMAN

FOREWORD BY
GERMAINE GREER

RIZZOLI
NEW YORK

First published in the United States of America in 2007 by
Rizzoli International Publications, Inc.
300 Park Avenue South
New York, NY 10010
www.rizzoliusa.com

Designed by Liz Workman

Dust jacket front and slipcase front show Dr Johnson's doorknob,
the first floor landing, Dr Johnson's House
Dust jacket back shows Washington Irving's mirror,
the bedroom, Sunnyside
Slipcase back shows George Washington's bed, Mount Vernon

Down House photographs © English Heritage
Carlyle House and Chartwell photographs © The National Trust

Printed in China

2007 2008 2009 2010 / 10 9 8 7 6 5 4 3 2 1

ISBN-10: 0-8478-2970-7
ISBN-13: 978-0-8478-2970-5

Library of Congress Catalog Number:
2007922645

Contents

London, happily, is becoming full of great men's houses, bought for the nation and preserved entire with the chairs they sat on and the cups they drank from, their umbrellas and their chests of drawers. And it is no frivolous curiosity that sends us to Dickens's house and Johnson's house and Carlyle's house and Keats's house. We know them from their houses...

−Virginia Woolf, *Great Men's Houses*, 1931

FOREWORD

The world is full of shrines, not all of them dedicated to Great Men. Some are dedicated to gods, some to goddesses, some to saints and some to warriors, and some to animal avatars of the gods. Some are no more than groups of stones, stained with ochre or bindi, or greasy with butterfat; others are huge and complex edifices, towering over a bone-chip of the Buddha or a thorn from Christ's crown. The very name 'shrine' means a container for something precious. Sometimes, when a beloved child meets an untimely death, the bereaved mother makes a shrine of the child's room, keeping it just as it was at the time of the calamity, as if expecting the missing one to return and take on life again. This is what we do with the houses of Great Men. We leave their pens in the ink-stand, their pipes in their ashtrays, their slippers under their beds, as if life were unbearable without the illusion of their presence. Wherever we find shrines we find superstition, self-deception and confabulation. The faithful, who will travel many miles to experience the fantasy nearness of the charismatic dead, are there to be gulled. After the money the pilgrims have spent and the distance they have traveled it would be cruel to jolt them with unvarnished truth.

The impulse to venerate is as old as humanity. When humans had nothing else to venerate they endowed rocks or waterholes or trees with divine power and treated them with reverence. Sacred animals were approached with awe and propitiated with gifts and sacrifices. When holy men and prophets arose among us, we struggled to get close to them, to touch them and to get their blessing. We craved locks of their hair, scraps of their raiment, which we held as lucky charms, if not actually miraculous. Christ is supposed to have left us no fewer than eighteen messianic foreskins. The fragments of the true cross eventually became so numerous that the enemies of the church said you could build a whole navy out of them. After Buddha was cremated, his remains were distributed to ten centres, each of which is supposed to have erected a stupa over them. All but one of the original stupas has disappeared, while fragments no bigger than crumbs are preserved in jewelled shrines in China, Tibet, Thailand, Myanmar, Sri Lanka, and India.

In the Cathedral of Bom Jesus in Goa, the embalmed body of the Jesuit missionary Francis Xavier can be seen dimly through the glass walls of a sarcophagus on top of a side altar, out of reach of the clutching hands of the faithful. When the cadaver was first exposed in Goa in 1556, a female devotee bit off the little toe of the right foot, which is missing to this day. Eventually the papal authorities demanded hard evidence that the saint's body had escaped the usual processes of decay, so part of the right arm was cut off and sent to Rome to be preserved in a reliquary in the church of the Gesu. A year later, the viscera were removed and distributed to Jesuit foundations all over the world. Every ten years or so the corpse is exposed to the public who throng in their millions to kiss it, and to buy amulets, rosaries, cards, and holy pictures that "have been touched to the body." Piety means profit.

The cult of Francis Xavier is alive and well, though those of us who are not Catholics might think we had grown out of such gross superstition. We do not now venerate saints or expect to be cured of what ails us by hanging fragments chipped from the skeletons of saints about our necks. Catholics may make vast shrines on the scale of Lourdes or Fatima or Knock and flock from all corners of the globe to be blessed or cured or inspired or unutterably depressed by such places. People who fancy

themselves more rational make shrines to Great Men. The people who fly to Dublin and make straight for the Martello Tower that is the setting for the beginning of *Ulysses*, and trudge around the streets of Dublin for days covering every site mentioned in any novel of James Joyce, believe themselves to be behaving sensibly. Joyce meant to eternise his Dublin; nobody would be more amused than he to think that much of his Dublin has been saved from the wrecker's ball to eternise him. Superstition dies hard.

Ever since Chaucer it has been true that as soon as April brings its sweet showers, folk long to go on pilgrimages. Pilgrimages always meant big money for the innkeepers, victuallers, ostlers, farriers, and chandlers who attended the faithful on their way; now they mean big money for tour operators. Lesser mortals make pilgrimages to the places where their favourite movies were shot; being in a movie, any movie, will bump up tourist revenue by more than half. The otherwise obscure town of Matamata in the North Island of New Zealand (population 6,000) has experienced a tourism boom since it was the chosen location for Tolkien's Hobbiton in the film trilogy of *The Lord of the Rings* and now caters for 300,000 visitors a year. Similarly Krakow and Kazimierz earn money from pilgrims to the scenes of *Schindler's List*. A third of a million people annually visit Salzburg so that they can inhabit the locations of *The Sound of Music*. J. K. Rowling fans have swarmed over Gloucester Cathedral, Alnwick Castle and the North Yorkshire Moors Railway, in search of Hogwarts.

Older and richer pilgrims prefer to display their level of literary culture by visiting places associated with literary icons, who are, nearly all of them, Great Men. There are a few shrines to Great Women but they are not kept up in the same spirit.

LEFT: JOHN KEATS'S MANTELPIECE, THE CHESTER ROOM, KEATS HOUSE

FOREWORD

For five pounds you can visit the cottage at Chawton where Jane Austen lived from 1809 till her death; eight dollars will get you a glimpse of Emily Dickinson's bedroom. Hill Top Farm, home of Beatrix Potter, recently recreated for a major motion picture, is too small to accomodate more than three coach parties a day. There is a timed entry system, but vistors may not buy tickets in advance. In these modest dwellings there is nothing designated Jane Austen's chair or Charlotte Brontë's desk, because these women did not have property or even a space of their own. What is unmistakeable about Chawton and Haworth and the Dickinson homestead is that they did not belong to the Great Women who have made them places of pilgrimage. With Great Men it is different; the entire space of even the vastest house is imagined as their own, even rooms they didn't enter from one year's end to another. Winston Churchill is thought to have pervaded Chartwell, so that every bibelot is where it is by his express command. In fact it was Clementine who ran Chartwell as a living breathing house full of visitors and children and animals, and I wouldn't mind betting that Winston could never find anything without asking her first where it was. But the pilgrimage demands a shrine unencumbered by any but the manes of the Great Man. So Springwood is declared the home of F. D. Roosevelt, as if Eleanor Roosevelt, called by Harry Truman the First Lady of the World, were not lying in the rose garden beside him.

When a woman takes a camera into a shrine dedicated to a Great Man, she is like a girl-child trespassing in her father's study. Nothing must be moved. Books may not be taken down and read, drawers must not be opened, chairs must not be sat on, finger marks may not be left on highly polished surfaces. Her attention is directed to important objects, but she notices irrelevancies, a splash of sunshine on the Turkey rug, a dust devil under the sofa, a fly buzzing against a windowpane. She doesn't push past through the shoulders of pushier people to get a view of just what the guide is talking about, but gazes at a skirting board instead. The tour guide goes through her patter, but the camera-child does not heed. She is looking at the doorknob and thinking subversive thoughts. Surely Dr Johnson's doorknob is just a doorknob? And is it even the knob that was on the door when Johnson was around to open and close it? Tetty Johnson died while Johnson lived at 17 Gough Square, and Johnson responded by going into a serious depression, wandering sleeplessly about London for nights on end. The house was run for the most part by the blind poetess Anna Williams who, when she presided over the tea-table, could only tell when to stop pouring when the hot fluid touched the black thumbnail she inserted in the cup. No wonder Reynolds preferred to bring his own cup along. Then there was the collapsed prostitute Johnson found in the gutter and brought into the house on his back, and the freed slave who kept running away, and Hodge the cat, all of whom had more to do with the doorknob than Johnson, who hid out most of the time he wasn't up in the garret sweating on the Dictionary at the well-run house of Hester Thrale. Gough Square is meant to feel as if Johnson dwelt there alone, attended by angels who kept everything spotless and in its place. When Johnson lived there, it was more like pandemonium.

Most of the houses in this book were inhabited and run by women, whose influence has been obliterated by history. The bed in Edgar Allen Poe Cottage is the one that Virginia Poe died in, yet here it is, Edgar Allen Poe's bed. Through most of the houses in this book stalk invisible wives, who can claim nothing, be they brilliant Jane Welsh Carlyle, or tipsy Tetty Johnson, or even Maria Bartow Cole whose bachelor uncle's house, Cedar Grove, actually was where she lived with her three sisters before her marriage in 1836 and after her husband's death in 1848. At Mount Vernon and Springwood, the wives are physically present for they are buried with their husbands in the grounds, but they are no more visible than Jefferson's wife, who died in 1782 in

FOREWORD

the tenth year of her married life. Jefferson is then supposed to have taken her slave half-sister as his concubine and had children with her, but nothing at Monticello records their existence. Elizabeth Smith Soane left no mark on Pitshanger Manor, which, though it was intended as a home for her two sons with John Soane and was built with her money, was sold six years after her husband had finished transforming it to his own taste. At Doughty Street a display case holds a few trifles that belonged to Catherine Hogarth Dickens, two lace handkerchiefs, two rings, a visiting-card case and an overmantel she embroidered. Catherine was abandoned. Adele Foucher Hugo ran away, leaving the house in the Place des Vosges to her husband and his whores. Samuel Morse arrived at Locust Grove aged fifty-five with no wife and three children in 1847; within a year he found a mistress for the house, his twenty-five-year-old deaf second cousin, Sarah Griswold Morse, who bore him four more children. She outlived him by nearly thirty years but left no mark upon his shrine, which she rented out after his death. Emma Darwin lived at Down House as a widow for fourteen years, but her house is her husband's, not hers. Martha Bernays Freud lived at Maresfield Gardens for twelve years after the death of her husband who was only there for a year before he died. Of all eighteen houses featured in this book only four, Sunnyside, Keats House, Leighton House, and Water House (the Morris Gallery) are not haunted by the wandering shade of a forgotten home-maker.

Germaine Greer
2007

LEFT: FRANKLIN DELANO ROOSEVELT'S BANISTERS, SPRINGWOOD

CHAPTER I

GREAT MEN'S
DOORKNOBS

RIGHT:

FRANKLIN DELANO ROOSEVELT'S DOORKNOB
THE BEDROOM, SPRINGWOOD

＊

OVERLEAF:

SAMUEL MORSE'S DOORKNOBS
THE ENTRANCE HALL AND THE BILLIARDS ROOM, LOCUST GROVE

CHARLES DICKENS'S DOORKNOB
THE DRAWING ROOM, THE CHARLES DICKENS MUSEUM

WASHINGTON IRVING'S DOORKNOB
THE LANDING, SUNNYSIDE

Sir Winston Churchill's Doorknob
The Uniform Room, Chartwell

EDGAR ALLAN POE'S DOORKNOB
THE HALL, EDGAR ALLAN POE COTTAGE

THOMAS COLE'S DOORKNOB
THE WEST BEDROOM, CEDAR GROVE

CHARLES DARWIN'S DOORKNOB

THE BEDROOM, DOWN HOUSE

CHAPTER II

Great Men's
CROCKERY

PREVIOUS PAGE:

SIR JOSHUA REYNOLDS'S CUP

THE ANNA WILLIAMS ROOM, DR JOHNSON'S HOUSE

✳

RIGHT:

VICTOR HUGO'S SOUP TUREEN

THE CHINESE DRAWING ROOM, MAISON DE VICTOR HUGO

CHARLES DARWIN'S SOUP TUREEN
THE DINING ROOM, DOWN HOUSE

Thomas Cole's Crockery
The Kitchen, Cedar Grove

CHARLES DICKENS'S CUP AND SAUCER
THE DINING ROOM, THE CHARLES DICKENS MUSEUM

RIGHT:

SIGMUND FREUD'S ASHTRAY
THE LANDING, THE FREUD MUSEUM

✳

OVERLEAF:

WASHINGTON IRVING'S DINNER SERVICE
THE DINING ROOM, SUNNYSIDE

JOHN KEATS'S BOWL

THE SITTING ROOM, KEATS HOUSE

EDGAR ALLAN POE'S SOUP TUREEN
THE PARLOUR, EDGAR ALLAN POE COTTAGE

WILLIAM MORRIS'S CUP AND SAUCER
THE DRAWING ROOM, WILLIAM MORRIS GALLERY

CHARLES DICKENS
Copied by Malcolm Stewart from the portrait by
ARY SCHEFFER, 1855, in National Portrait Gallery
Presented 1929 by Sir CHARLES CHEERS WAKEFIELD Bart. C.B.E.

CHAPTER III

GREAT MEN'S
MANTELPIECES

CHARLES DICKENS'S MANTELPIECE
THE STUDY, THE CHARLES DICKENS MUSEUM

✳

THOMAS JEFFERSON'S MANTELPIECE
THE DINING ROOM, MONTICELLO

SIGMUND FREUD'S MANTELPIECE
THE LIBRARY, THE FREUD MUSEUM

GEORGE WASHINGTON'S MANTELPIECE
THE SMALL DINING ROOM, MOUNT VERNON

RIGHT:

DR JOHNSON'S MANTELPIECE
THE ANNE WILLIAMS ROOM, DR JOHNSON'S HOUSE

✳

OVERLEAF:

THOMAS CARLYLE'S MANTLEPIECES
THE DRAWING ROOM AND THE STUDY, CARLYLE'S HOUSE

SIR WINSTON CHURCHILL'S MANTELPIECE

THE DRAWING ROOM, CHARTWELL

CHARLES DARWIN'S MANTELPIECE
THE DRAWING ROOM, DOWN HOUSE

Frederic, Lord Leighton's Mantelpiece
The Studio, Leighton House Museum

FRANKLIN DELANO ROOSEVELT'S MANTELPIECE

THE BEDROOM, SPRINGWOOD

CHAPTER IV

Great Men's
CHAIRS

THOMAS JEFFERSON'S CHAIR
THE CABINET, MONTICELLO

*

OVERLEAF, LEFT:

FRANKLIN DELANO ROOSEVELT'S CHAIR
THE LIVING ROOM, SPRINGWOOD

OVERLEAF, RIGHT:

SIR WINSTON CHURCHILL'S CHAIR
THE STUDY, CHARTWELL

·

GEORGE WASHINGTON'S CHAIR
THE STUDY, MOUNT VERNON

FREDERIC, LORD LEIGHTON'S CHAIR
THE SILK ROOM, LEIGHTON HOUSE MUSEUM

RIGHT:

THOMAS COLE'S CHAIR

THE WEST PARLOUR, CEDAR GROVE

✳

OVERLEAF:

SIGMUND FREUD'S CHAIRS

THE LANDING AND THE STUDY, THE FREUD MUSEUM

WASHINTON IRVING'S CHAIR
THE BEDROOM, SUNNYSIDE

EDGAR ALLAN POE'S CHAIR
THE PARLOUR, EDGAR ALLAN POE COTTAGE

CHAPTER V

GREAT MEN'S
DESKS

PREVIOUS PAGE:

WASHINGTON IRVING'S DESK

THE STUDY, SUNNYSIDE

*

RIGHT:

CHARLES DARWIN'S DESK

THE STUDY, DOWN HOUSE

CHARLES DICKENS'S DESK
THE STUDY, THE CHARLES DICKENS MUSEUM

SIGMUND FREUD'S DESK
THE STUDY, THE FREUD MUSEUM

RIGHT:

THOMAS CARLYLE'S DESK

THE STUDY, CARLYLE'S HOUSE

❋

OVERLEAF:

SIR WINSTON CHURCHILL'S DESK

THE STUDY, CHARTWELL

THOMAS JEFFERSON'S DESK
THE CABINET, MONTICELLO

VICTOR HUGO'S DESK
THE BEDROOM, MAISON DE VICTOR HUGO

FRANKLIN DELANO ROOSEVELT'S DESK
THE STUDY, SPRINGWOOD

D

VICKI BAUM
DAS GROSSE
EINMALEINS

FLEURON EIN WINTER IM JÄGERHOFE

HERMYNIA
ZUR MÜHL
DAS RIESEN
RAD

Dickens
Weihnachts-
geschichten

LAGERLÖF
CHRISTUS-
LEGENDEN

Ernst
Zahn

BAR-
CHESTER
TOWER

ANTHONY
TROLLOPE

RAINER MARIA RILKE

NCE
LADY
NETS
S Y

CHAPTER VI

GREAT MEN'S
BOOKS

PREVIOUS PAGE:

SIGMUND FREUD'S BOOKS

THE LANDING, THE FREUD MUSEUM

RIGHT:

CHARLES DARWIN'S BOOKS

THE DRAWING ROOM, DOWN HOUSE

SIGMUND FREUD'S BOOKS
THE STUDY, THE FREUD MUSEUM

THOMAS COLE'S BOOKS
THE WEST PARLOUR, CEDAR GROVE

✻

FRANKLIN DELANO ROOSEVELT'S BOOKS
THE LIVING ROOM, SPRINGWOOD

the
key

patricia
wentworth

THERE SHALL BE NO NIGHT

ROBERT E. SH...

THE WORKERS AT WAR

FRANK JULIAN WARNE

Century New World Series

AMERICAN PLANNING AND CIVIC ANNUAL

1935

...LLA... & R.J. YEATM...

NEW
FRONTIERS
OF THE
MIND

J. B. RHINE

THE
BUNDLE
OF
LIFE

BURKE

NEW
YEAR'S
DAY

EDITH
WHARTON

THE
OLD
MAID

EDITH
WHARTON

THE
SPARK

RESPONSE

MARY
POWNALL BROMET

WASHINGTON IRVING'S BOOKS
THE STUDY, SUNNYSIDE

Thomas Jefferson's Books
The Book Room, Monticello

SIR WINSTON CHURCHILL'S BOOKS
THE STUDY, CHARTWELL

CHAPTER VII

Great Men's
BANISTERS

PREVIOUS PAGE:

WILLIAM MORRIS'S BANISTERS
WILLIAM MORRIS GALLERY

✴

RIGHT:

VICTOR HUGO'S BANISTERS
MAISON DE VICTOR HUGO

CHARLES DARWIN'S BANISTERS
DOWN HOUSE

RIGHT:

Dr Johnson's Banisters

Dr Johnson's House

*

OVERLEAF:

Frederic, Lord Leighton's Banisters

Leighton House Museum

CHARLES DICKENS'S BANISTERS
THE CHARLES DICKENS MUSEUM

Thomas Carlyle's Banisters
Carlyle's House

Sir John Soane's Banisters

Pitshanger Manor

✳

George Washington's Banisters

Mount Vernon

SIGMUND FREUD'S BANISTERS
THE FREUD MUSEUM

Sir Winston Churchill's Banisters

Chartwell

CHAPTER VIII

Great Men's
Mirrors

CHARLES DARWIN'S MIRROR

THE BILLIARD ROOM, DOWN HOUSE

RIGHT:

WASHINGTON IRVING'S MIRROR

THE BEDROOM, SUNNYSIDE

FRANKLIN DELANO ROOSEVELT'S MIRROR
THE BEDROOM, SPRINGWOOD

✳

CHARLES DICKENS'S MIRRORS
THE BEDROOM AND THE DRAWING ROOM, THE CHARLES DICKENS MUSEUM

SIGMUND FREUD'S MIRROR
THE LANDING, THE FREUD MUSEUM

JOHN KEATS'S MIRROR
THE CHESTER ROOM, KEATS HOUSE

EDGAR ALLAN POE'S MIRROR
THE PARLOUR, EDGAR ALLAN POE COTTAGE

THOMAS COLE'S MIRROR
THE WEST BEDROOM, CEDAR GROVE

CHAPTER IX

GREAT MEN'S
SKIRTING BOARDS

THOMAS CARLYLE'S SKIRTING BOARD
THE DRAWING ROOM, CARLYLE'S HOUSE

✳

VICTOR HUGO'S SKIRTING BOARD
SALON DU RETOUR D'EXIL, MAISON DE VICTOR HUGO

DR JOHNSON'S SKIRTING BOARD
THE LIBRARY, DR JOHNSON'S HOUSE

SIR WINSTON CHURCHILL'S SKIRTING BOARD
THE LANDING, CHARTWELL

*

FREDERIC, LORD LEIGHTON'S SKIRTING BOARDS
THE DINING ROOM AND THE SILK ROOM, LEIGHTON HOUSE MUSEUM

GEORGE WASHINGTON'S SKIRTING BOARD
THE STUDY, MOUNT VERNON

SIR JOHN SOANE'S SKIRTING BOARD
THE BEDROOM, PITSHANGER MANOR

RIGHT:

FRANKLIN DELANO ROOSEVELT's SKIRTING BOARD
THE BEDROOM, SPRINGWOOD

OVERLEAF, LEFT:

SIGMUND FREUD's SKIRTING BOARD
THE BEDROOM, THE FREUD MUSEUM

OVERLEAF, RIGHT:

CHARLES DARWIN's SKIRTING BOARD
THE DRAWING ROOM, DOWN HOUSE

SAMUEL MORSE'S SKIRTING BOARD
THE DRAWING ROOM, LOCUST GROVE

CHAPTER X

GREAT MEN'S
BEDS

PREVIOUS PAGE:

THOMAS COLE'S BED

THE WEST BEDROOM, CEDAR GROVE

*

RIGHT:

FRANKLIN DELANO ROOSEVELT'S BED

THE BEDROOM, SPRINGWOOD

EDGAR ALLAN POE'S BED
THE BEDROOM, EDGAR ALLAN POE COTTAGE

WASHINGTON IRVING'S BED

THE BEDROOM, SUNNYSIDE

RIGHT:

FREDERIC, LORD LEIGHTON'S BED
THE BEDROOM, LEIGHTON HOUSE MUSEUM

✳

OVERLEAF:

THOMAS JEFFERSON'S BED
THE BED CHAMBER, MONTICELLO

GEORGE WASHINGTON'S BED
THE BEDROOM, MOUNT VERNON

INDEX OF
GREAT MEN'S HOUSES

THOMAS CARLYLE'S HOUSE
CARLYLE'S HOUSE
24 CHEYNE ROW, CHELSEA,
LONDON SW3 5HL
TELEPHONE: +44 207 352 7087

WINSTON CHURCHILL'S HOUSE
CHARTWELL
MAPLETON ROAD, WESTERHAM,
KENT TN16 1PS
TELEPHONE: +44 1732 868 381

THOMAS COLE'S HOUSE
CEDAR GROVE
218 SPRING STREET,
CATSKILL, NY 12414
TELEPHONE: 518 943 7465

CHARLES DARWIN'S HOUSE
DOWN HOUSE,
LUXTED ROAD, DOWNE,
KENT BR6 7JT
TELEPHONE: +44 1689 859 119

THE CHARLES DICKENS MUSEUM
48 DOUGHTY STREET
LONDON WC1N 2LX
TELEPHONE: +44 207 405 2127

THE FREUD MUSEUM
20 MARESFIELD GARDENS,
LONDON NW3 5SX
TELEPHONE: +44 207 435 2002

MAISON DE VICTOR HUGO
6, PLACE DES VOSGES,
4ᵀᴴ ARRONDISSEMENT
75004 PARIS
TELEPHONE: +33 1 42 72 10 16

WASHINGTON IRVING'S HOUSE
SUNNYSIDE
89 WEST SUNNYSIDE LANE,
TARRYTOWN, NY 10591
TELEPHONE: 914 591 8763

THOMAS JEFFERSON'S HOUSE
MONTICELLO
600 COLLEGE DRIVE,
CHARLOTTESVILLE, VA 22902
TELEPHONE: 434 984 9822

DR. JOHNSON'S HOUSE
17 GOUGH SQUARE,
LONDON EC4A 3DE
TELEPHONE: +44 207 353 3745

JOHN KEATS'S HOUSE
KEATS HOUSE
KEATS GROVE,
LONDON, NW3 2RR
TELEPHONE: +44 207 435 2062

FREDERIC, LORD LEIGHTON'S HOUSE
LEIGHTON HOUSE MUSEUM
12 HOLLAND PARK ROAD,
LONDON, W14 8LZ
TELEPHONE: +44 207 602 3316

WILLIAM MORRIS'S HOUSE
WILLIAM MORRIS GALLERY
LLOYD PARK, FOREST ROAD,
LONDON E17 4PP
TELEPHONE: +44 208 527 3782

SAMUEL MORSE'S HOUSE
LOCUST GROVE,
2683 SOUTH ROAD,
POUGHKEEPSIE, NY 12601
TELEPHONE: 845 454 4500

EDGAR ALLAN POE'S HOUSE
EDGAR ALLAN POE COTTAGE
2640 GRAND CONCOURSE,
NEW YORK. NY 10458
TELEPHONE: 718 881 8900

FRANKLIN DELANO ROOSEVELT'S HOUSE
SPRINGWOOD
4097 ALBANY POST ROAD,
HYDE PARK, NY 12538
TELEPHONE: 800 337 8474

SIR JOHN SOANE'S HOUSE
PITSHANGER MANOR
WALPOLE PARK, MATTOCK LANE,
LONDON W5 5EQ
TELEPHONE: +44 208 567 1227

GEORGE WASHINGTON'S HOUSE
MOUNT VERNON
3200 MOUNT VERNON MEMORIAL HIGHWAY,
MOUNT VERNON, VA 22121
TELEPHONE: 703 799 8691